IMAGES
of America

BALTIMORE
in WORLD WAR II

Members of the Maryland Home Guard present the colors at Pimlico in 1942. (Courtesy Library of Congress, FSA-OWI Collection.)

IMAGES
of America

BALTIMORE
in WORLD WAR II

William M. Armstrong

ARCADIA
PUBLISHING

Published by Arcadia Publishing
Charleston SC, Chicago IL, Portsmouth NH, San Francisco CA

Printed in the United States of America

Library of Congress Catalog Card Number: 2005928476

For all general information contact Arcadia Publishing at:
Telephone 843-853-2070
Fax 843-853-0044
E-mail sales@arcadiapublishing.com
For customer service and orders:
Toll-Free 1-888-313-2665

Visit us on the Internet at www.arcadiapublishing.com

Security of America's ports during the war rested primarily with the U.S. Coast Guard. The first port security school was established early in the war at Fort McHenry under the direction of the Captain of the Port, Baltimore. Some graduates would see duty in Baltimore, monitoring harbor traffic and guarding shipyards and vital military depot areas. Courses included coverage of munitions, fire hazards, sabotage, and law enforcement. This class is posing with three of Fort McHenry's Rodman guns on November 11, 1942. (Courtesy the National Park Service, Fort McHenry National Monument and Historic Shrine.)

CONTENTS

ACKNOWLEDGMENTS

This book is dedicated to the Baltimoreans who helped win the war and to Melanie, who reintroduced me to a city I only thought I knew.

Nothing in this book would have been possible without two important groups of people: those who created a pictorial record of these important events and those who had the foresight to preserve those records. The photographs contained herein are the work of many different photographers—many unnamed and others quite well known.

I am particularly indebted to the photographers of the Farm Security Administration Office of War Information (FSA-OWI), who took photographs of various activities across the country, including Baltimore, as well as overseas. Their work is scattered throughout every chapter. Alfred Palmer chronicled the first Liberty ships at Curtis Bay and Bethlehem-Fairfield. Arthur Siegel went back to Fairfield in 1943, covering the ships and the workers who built them. Roger Smith also covered Fairfield in 1943 during the building of the SS *Frederick Douglass*; his work includes this book's cover photo. John Vachon covered the Bethlehem Steel plant at Sparrows Point. Howard Liberman covered the Glenn L. Martin Company in 1942, particularly its plant in Canton and the carpool operation at Middle River. Marjory Collins covered commuters, traffic jams, and public transportation, as well as city life. Ann Rosener covered Holabird Quartermaster Depot, while Danish covered the process of scrap-steel recycling. These images came from the records of the Office of War Information at the National Archives in College Park, Maryland, and from the FSA-OWI Collection of the Library of Congress, Prints and Photographs Division.

Coverage of industry, military facilities, and overseas service was also provided by the U.S. Navy, Coast Guard, Army Signal Corps, and Army Corps of Engineers. Present in quantity are some of the excellent aerial shots taken by crews from Naval Air Station Anacostia. These and other official photographs were provided by the National Archives in College Park.

For their assistance in obtaining photographs, I would especially like to thank Jason Williams and the staff of the Still Pictures Branch, National Archives and Records Administration (NARA) at College Park; Stan Piet of the Glenn L. Martin Maryland Aviation Museum; Ranger Vince Vaise of the National Park Service, Fort McHenry National Monument and Historic Shrine; the staff of the Dundalk–Patapsco Neck Historical Society; the Prints and Photographs Division of the Library of Congress (LoC); Karen Anson of the Franklin Delano Roosevelt Library; Bonnie Burlbaw and Karen Finch of the George H. W. Bush Presidential Library; David Prencipe and the staff of the Maryland Historical Society in Baltimore; and George Shriner Jr.

In addition, a number of individuals have provided assistance ranging from sage advice to editorial comment. I would particularly like to thank my colleagues Mike Reis, Ken Durr, and Garry Adelman for their thoughts and suggestions, as well as Ian Warthin and Eva Heinzen, who kept a watchful eye for the absurd and the intriguing. Paul Cora of the Baltimore Maritime Museum provided leads regarding Curtis Bay and the 353rd Fighter Group. Numerous other individuals have given feedback regarding the photos and captions. My special thanks to Lewis Boulanger, who, I am convinced, can fix anything with a microprocessor in it. My thanks to all of you, and I hope that I have done your efforts justice.

INTRODUCTION

This book is a snapshot of part of Baltimore's war effort as it was recorded at the time. In scope, it covers the entire Baltimore metropolitan area as we know it today, encompassing both the city and its immediate suburbs, places with Baltimore addresses where people from across the city went to work. I have devoted special sections to the building of Liberty ships and aircraft, as these were the two largest sources of employment during the war. It could not be, and is not, exhaustive. For those who do not remember Baltimore as it was during World War II, the author hopes to convey some idea of the city's contributions to victory. Hopefully those who do remember will find this collection of photos to be a fitting tribute to the city and its people. The author has attempted to make available photos that have been tucked away for decades, or that have never before been published, as well as some immediately recognizable images.

Marylanders are fortunate to have a variety of historical resources documenting the state's wartime history. By far the best single resource is the four-volume series *Maryland in World War II*, published by the War Records Division of the Maryland Historical Society during the 1950s. These volumes are based on historical accounts by Baltimore's military, commercial, and community organizations. They have been drawn from heavily by the author for accounts of military and industrial activities as well as the history of Baltimore's civil defenses. The *Baltimore Sun* is also an invaluable source of information, and wartime issues have been preserved on microfilm. Other notable works are included in the bibliography.

Baltimore has been described as a somewhat sleepy Southern city as it entered the 1930s, comparatively light on manufacturing and deeply segregated. Industry was expanding, largely in satellite operations controlled by out-of-state interests: Bethlehem Steel, Revere, Rheem, Koppers, General Motors, Bendix, Westinghouse, and Western Electric. The city had a long tradition of shipbuilding dating back beyond the days of the Baltimore clippers, and yards operated by Bethlehem Steel and Maryland Drydock continued that tradition. Then came aviation, beginning with names like Curtiss-Caproni and Berliner-Joyce. When pioneer aviator and industrialist Glenn Martin decided to move his growing aircraft business from Cleveland, he chose Baltimore. The Glenn L. Martin Company not only brought a hi-tech industry to the city, it was also one of few large firms to be based here. With the coming of war, it would be these industries that spearheaded Baltimore's civilian war effort. In any given year between 1942 and 1945, well over 60,000 Baltimoreans were working in shipyards, while by 1943, over 53,000 worked at Martin.

Baltimore's military participation was also notable. Though none of the city's facilities were particularly large, all played important roles during the war. Many Baltimoreans served in the military and saw duty in just about every corner of the globe. Baltimore contributed heavily to one of the most famous U.S. Army divisions to serve in the war, the 29th Infantry, elements of which were headquartered downtown in peacetime, as well as every other major military organization in every branch of national service.

Meanwhile, the city itself seemed to be in danger. After Pearl Harbor, a series of "confirmed" reports, verified by the army and navy, told of "unfriendly" aircraft over the California coast!

(This never occurred, we now know.) Fear of air raids, probably unjustified, was as real as in London. Fear of sabotage, probably justified, kept security personnel at strategic points all across the city. With the coming of war, even the trivial seemed deadly serious—such as the realization that the city's gas lamps could not be quickly snuffed during a blackout.

The following pages offer a glimpse into that era, when the entire city came together with one purpose: to achieve ultimate victory.

One

LIFE IN WARTIME
BALTIMORE

The western half of downtown Baltimore is shown as it appeared at the outbreak of hostilities. The old Baltimore Trust Building is near center, while Baltimore City Hall, the Municipal Building, the War Memorial, and the Shot Tower are all visible at upper right. The harbor area was fairly industrialized, with many of today's popular pleasure spots being devoted to maritime endeavors such as shipbuilding and fitting. (Courtesy NARA.)

The German cruiser *Emden* is shown docked alongside Broadway Pier in Fells Point on April 22, 1936, during its controversial 10-day official visit to the city. Sponsored by the 76 German-American societies in Baltimore, the crew of the *Emden* was welcomed by Baltimore mayor Howard Jackson, Maryland governor Herbert O'Conor, and even the U.S. Naval Academy, while thousands of Baltimoreans waited hours for tours of the warship. The visit stirred fierce protests, however, led by Baltimore's Jewish community and a host of religious leaders, academics, and political officials—a situation no doubt made worse by reports that the crew had celebrated Hitler's birthday with full Nazi pomp in the Chesapeake Bay while en route. The American Legion abandoned plans to greet the vessel with a musical performance, while 300 city police were placed on 12-hour shifts known as "*Emden* Duty" to ward off any violent protest. (Courtesy NARA.)

It could be argued that America was hardly neutral during the fall of 1941. There was great concern that Britain would not be able to sustain the Nazi onslaught, and from many quarters a strong desire to aid Britain in any way possible was voiced. The Committee to Defend America sponsored a series of rallies called "Battle of the Atlantic Week," the Baltimore event consisting of an evening parade and a rally outside the War Memorial Building. The purpose of these rallies was to gain support for a stronger response against German aggression. Mayor Jackson and Governor O'Conor both called for participation in the event, and Mayor Jackson addressed the rally. This group is preparing to march in the parade, carrying the flags of friendly nations—including Poland, Britain, China, and Free France. The parade was decidedly anti-Nazi, with floats showcasing the German government's atrocities against innocents across Europe. (Courtesy the Maryland Historical Society.)

The Baltimore Trust Building was still the distinguishing feature of the city's skyline when this photo was taken of the Inner Harbor. The harbor had yet to develop into a center for tourism and retail. This sort of placid atmosphere would be severely interrupted by the attack on Pearl Harbor, as the city struggled to prepare itself for war. (Courtesy NARA.)

The view up Charles Street to Mount Vernon Place and the Washington Monument looks much the same as it does today, save for the relatively sparse vehicular traffic. (Courtesy NARA.)

This view, looking south down Charles Street, was probably taken from atop the Washington Monument. Many of these buildings are still standing, though the skyline in the distance has changed quite a bit. (Courtesy NARA.)

When war came, rubber was quickly rationed in all its forms, including shoe soles. Not to worry, says the reassuring sign at the Selis Company's shop. Recycling was a key feature of civilian participation in the war effort. (Courtesy LoC, FSA-OWI Collection.)

The message on this bus window was part of a campaign to force participation in air-raid drills and warning procedures, which not everyone in the country took seriously. Still, while it might seem far-fetched today, the threat of enemy air attack during the war was perceived as quite real by many, and Baltimore adopted a more or less standard array of defensive measures. (Courtesy LoC, FSA-OWI Collection.)

Passers-by examine one of Baltimore's curious new air-raid warning sirens, 80 of which went up in various locations around the city. This one is on St. Paul Street. The sirens were tied to the Baltimore Filter Center, which was manned by volunteers and overseen by the Army Air Forces. The sirens would be run based on information from Civil Defense Ground Observer Corps volunteers, who were airplane-spotting from towers and other vantage points as far away as the Eastern Shore. Early in the war, they would have alerted the 59th Fighter Squadron based at Martin Field in Middle River. Unfortunately, while the filter center went online two days after the Pearl Harbor attack, the sirens did not operate as planned and took some time to become operational. In any event, they were never needed. The filter center's duties passed to a Philadelphia regional center in October 1943, and the warning system was deactivated in 1945. (Courtesy the Maryland Historical Society.)

Perhaps more curious than the air-raid sirens were these sandbags stacked against the windows of city buildings, the value of which appears dubious in the event of an actual raid. After "confirmed" reports of enemy aircraft over California, civil-defense officials took no chances. Evacuation plans were drawn, and there was great concern that the city did not have enough air-raid shelters. (Courtesy the Maryland Historical Society.)

Early in the war, even the Municipal Building next to city hall was sporting sand bags intended to prevent a near-ground-level explosion from penetrating the building. Many of the defensive measures taken in the city were probably more of psychological benefit than anything else. (Courtesy LoC, FSA-OWI Collection.)

To further confuse would-be aerial attackers, dummy houses were erected along Eastern Boulevard; this one was constructed of pine, plywood, and fly screen. As it turned out, the only role played by the dummy houses was that of roadside curiosity, as no German aircraft ever visited the East Coast. (Courtesy NARA.)

A variety of materials were used for the multi-colored camouflage concealment at the Glenn L. Martin plant, including fly screen and fiberglass net. The camouflage pattern was visually repeated on the factory buildings. (Courtesy NARA.)

Employees at the Glenn L. Martin plant in Middle River walk to the factory from cars parked under camouflage netting, part of Baltimore's "passive defense" measures to thwart enemy aircraft. Neither Germany nor Japan possessed aircraft capable of reaching Baltimore from Axis territory during the war, but defensive measures such as this were adopted on both coasts of the United States. (Courtesy LoC, FSA-OWI Collection.)

The camouflage netting at the Martin plant was at one point doing far more harm than good, as a late-January 1943 snowstorm toppled support columns and crushed cars in the lot below. Employees set to head home were instead confronted with scenes like this one—the unfortunate automobile actually lifted off the ground on one side; the Maryland license tag reads "Drive Carefully." (Courtesy NARA.)

Winston Churchill and President Roosevelt are shown meeting in Washington on June 25, 1942. Due to return to Britain that evening, Churchill had chosen to fly a British-flagged clipper from Baltimore's Harbor Field Seaplane Terminal. The event gave rise to one of history's many "what-ifs," as British security agents subdued a crazed gunman threatening to "do in" the famous wartime leader. (Courtesy the Franklin D. Roosevelt Library.)

During the war, British Overseas Airways Corporation leased Baltimore's Harbor Field Seaplane Terminal from Pan American Airways, flying Boeing 314 clippers like the one in the foreground. It was here that Winston Churchill was threatened with assassination by a firearm-wielding local "crackpate" as he departed for Britain the evening of June 25, 1942. The incident is recounted by Churchill in his multi-volume epic *The Second World War*. (Courtesy the Maryland Historical Society.)

Blood donors file into the Red Cross Blood Donor Center at 8 South Charles Street to do their part in the war effort. The poster, which shows a medic tending to a wounded G.I., reads, "He gave his blood . . . Will you give yours?" Many Baltimoreans did. (Courtesy the Glenn L. Martin Maryland Aviation Museum.)

Workers gather at a mobile Baltimore Red Cross truck. The Baltimore Red Cross Blood Donor Center received the Army-Navy "E" Award for wartime efficiency, with two additional stars (each star marked an additional issuance of the annual "E" Award). (Courtesy the Glenn L. Martin Maryland Aviation Museum.)

Jean Finnegan of the Glenn L. Martin Company displays her "Gallon Club" membership plaque at a blood-donor appreciation ceremony in the 5th Regiment Armory in 1943. Sponsored by the Maryland Department of the 29th Division Association, the mahogany plaques were awarded to Marylanders who had donated a gallon or more of blood for the war effort–6,013 donors by war's end! Each featured the "Blue and Gray" division insignia and was inscribed in gold with the donor's name. There was also a recognized "Two-Gallon Club." Glenn Martin was a major sponsor of the program. (Courtesy the Glenn L. Martin Maryland Aviation Museum.)

The funding of World War II was in many ways a grass-roots effort. This patriotic leaflet put out by the Baltimore War and Community Fund encouraged donations of one hour's pay per month to support the USO, the War Relief Emergency Fund, and a host of local home-defense agencies. Starting in 1942, the fund raised a total of $10,440,454 for the war effort—meeting or beating every annual target. (Courtesy the Dundalk–Patapsco Neck Historical Society.)

These women at the Glenn L. Martin plant in Middle River are preparing to distribute war bonds to help fund the massive war effort. Baltimore contributed heavily to such campaigns and was per capita one of the highest contributing cities in America. (Courtesy the Glenn L. Martin Maryland Aviation Museum.)

Children contributed to the war effort in many ways. Here, students at Hamilton Junior High School are shown holding a canned food drive. (Courtesy the Maryland Historical Society.)

Using their Radio Flyer wagon, these two Dundalk boys have collected rubber scrap for the Salvage for Victory Campaign. When the Japanese invaded Southeast Asia, they cut off most of the world's supply of rubber. To keep a modern mechanized army supplied, the American war effort relied on recycled rubber for everything from tank treads to gas masks. (Courtesy the Dundalk–Patapsco Neck Historical Society.)

What a sight! Certainly one of the strangest items to ever make its way down Holliday Street, a disassembled B-26 Marauder, fresh from fierce combat in the Southwest Pacific, is being hauled to War Memorial Plaza in preparation for Hero Day on August 26, 1943. A crowd of passers-by has gathered as the plane sits across from city hall. (Courtesy the Glenn L. Martin Maryland Aviation Museum.)

Parked at War Memorial Plaza, the veteran B-26—complete with kill markings tallying its crew's successes against Japanese shipping—is the center of attention on Hero Day in 1943. Behind it is a mock-up of a navy destroyer. The War Memorial Building had been dedicated to veterans of World War I and quickly became a community focal point during World War II. (Courtesy the Glenn L. Martin Maryland Aviation Museum.)

"Experts covering the contest agreed it was the biggest game of this generation," wrote Jesse Linthicum of the *Baltimore Sun* of the 1944 Army-Navy Game. Held at Municipal Stadium on December 3, the event attracted a host of high military officials—and about 70,000 fans! The stadium was rebuilt after the war as Memorial Stadium. (Courtesy NARA.)

Even navy commander-in-chief Ernest J. King was in attendance at the 1944 Army-Navy Game; he is shown here shaking hands with other military officials on the field at Municipal Stadium. Unfortunately for Navy fans, it was the Army that walked out on top with a 23-7 win. Gen. George C. Marshall was there to savor the moment. Fourteen days later, King would be promoted to fleet admiral. (Courtesy NARA.)

Commuters hop on and off the trolleys that service the Bethlehem-Fairfield yard. Schools and businesses converted to staggered hours so that the constantly running transit vehicles would be able to handle travel volume. (Courtesy LoC, FSA-OWI Collection.)

This large crowd is waiting to board the "S"-route bus to Liberty Heights, and it does not look possible that they all made it on board. Buses and trolleys ran constantly during the war, as ridership increased exponentially over prewar volume. (Courtesy LoC, FSA-OWI Collection.)

Workers, mainly women, board the Number 10 trackless trolley to Roland Park. The trackless trolleys ran on rubber tires but did not use precious gasoline. They were powered by overhead electrical wires of the type quite familiar to modern rail commuters. (Courtesy LoC, FSA-OWI Collection.)

Workmen waiting for public transportation downtown check out the latest headlines. One of Baltimore's air-raid warning sirens is visible on the street corner at left in the background. (Courtesy LoC, FSA-OWI Collection.)

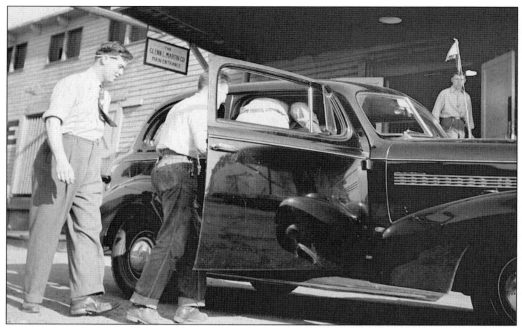

As one of the largest employers in the region, the Glenn L. Martin Company was able to save invaluable gasoline and conserve precious rubber tires by encouraging carpooling on a massive scale. Here a whole crowd is shown piling into a nicely polished sedan at the end of their shift. The company also encouraged the use of mass transit. (Courtesy LoC, FSA-OWI Collection.)

Stop—Marauder Crossing! A minor traffic backup is created when a brand-new B-26 is towed across Eastern Boulevard from Martin Plant Number 2 to the main runway and ramp. This procedure was a common sight to residents of Middle River during the war. (Courtesy the Glenn L. Martin Maryland Aviation Museum.)

This is obviously not a blackout night; crowds of shoppers and theatergoers flocked to Park and Lexington in the heart of the downtown shopping and entertainment scene. Kresge's five-and-dime and Ann Lewis seem to be doing good business, while the entertainment-minded are checking out *Happy Go Lucky* at Keith's Theater. (Courtesy LoC, FSA-OWI Collection.)

Movie theaters downtown stayed open late to draw in the night-shift workers. This crowd is in front of the New Theater on Lexington Street, one of numerous all-but-forgotten movie theaters in the downtown area. (Courtesy LoC, FSA-OWI Collection.)

"You wouldn't know the plant at Middle River and the village that is springing up here," Glenn Martin wrote acquaintances in September 1942. The need for housing for thousands of wartime workers, many from out of state, led the government to establish entire communities of temporary trailer houses such as this one. These publicity photos were meant to show a high quality of life. (Courtesy LoC, FSA-OWI Collection.)

In this publicity photo, a "typical" 1940s family shows that even a government-issue trailer can be home sweet home. Not all the housing developments were temporary, and wartime developments like Aero Acres and Victory Villa still exist today. Names like Altimeter Court and Cockpit Street mark the Martin communities in Middle River. (Courtesy LoC, FSA-OWI Collection.)

Two

BALTIMORE'S MILITARY FACILITIES

Known to locals as "Camp Holabird" (it only carried that name officially from 1918 to 1919), the bulk of activities at Holabird Quartermaster Depot during the early years of the war were centered around motor transport. In 1940, when the army recognized the need for a small, fast utility truck, they turned to the specialists at Holabird for a set of specifications and requirements. The end result was the jeep. (Courtesy NARA.)

Getting ready to run Holabird's obstacle course, Brig. Gen. Vernon Prichard is at the wheel of a Bantam BRC-40 still in use at Holabird in 1942. Bantam had been one of three competitors for the "jeep" contract, along with Willys and Ford, all of the designs having been tested at Holabird. Though the BRC-40 did not win, the winning Willys design was based heavily on it. (Courtesy NARA.)

Holabird had a treacherous vehicle obstacle course that recreated hazards such as mud, floodwater, steep inclines, and rocks. Here it appears that a driver is being put through his paces at the mudhole. In fact, the driver is Holabird's commanding officer, Col. (later Brig. Gen.) Herbert J. Lawes, giving a demonstration to Brig. Gen. Trelawney E. Marchant of the 30th Infantry Division. (Courtesy NARA.)

As the army expanded, so did the need to feed it, and these men were the first of the Quartermaster Corps' "90-Day Napoleons," shown here making meatballs for dinner. After completing the 90-day training period, "Napoleons" received commissions as second lieutenants. These students, who entered training just two months before Pearl Harbor, would soon be part of an unsung but vital component of the war effort. (Courtesy NARA.)

"The Army has a Popeye," reads the caption on this Signal Corps photograph taken at the Holabird Quartermaster Depot. With good humor, Mess Sgt. C. H. Snell of the depot poses with an appetizing load of spinach. Within a few short months, the graduates of the Quartermaster School would find themselves responsible for feeding hundreds of soldiers. (Courtesy NARA.)

Their instructor watches with an attentive eye as students at the Holabird Quartermaster Motor Transport School learn hands-on the fundamentals of vehicle transmissions. Three of the men are wearing the army's prewar M1938 fatigues, complete with floppy hats. Made of dark blue denim and designed more for rugged wear than concealment, the M1938 disappeared quickly after the start of the war. (Courtesy NARA.)

Women's Army Auxiliary Corps (WAAC) officers Eileen Knowler (left) and Jessie Hogan are learning the fundamentals of internal combustion engines at the Holabird Motor Transport School in 1942. They are part of an eight-woman class for WAAC officers. (Courtesy NARA.)

Later in the war, this could have been a view of the famous "Red Ball Express," but these are transport crews in training organizing a convoy at Holabird Quartermaster Depot. The Allies won with a fully mechanized military, and the ability to keep large convoys like this operating smoothly was absolutely critical in keeping rapidly moving forces supplied. (Courtesy LoC, FSA-OWI Collection.)

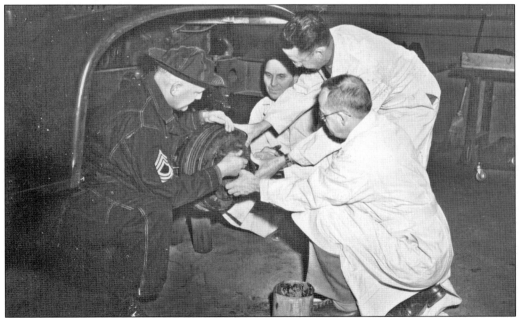

At Holabird, even generals learned maintenance! Here (clockwise from left) M.Sgt. George Winters teaches the basics of wheel upkeep to Brigadier Generals Vernon Prichard (4th Armored Division), Joseph Hutchinson (21st Infantry Division), and Trelawney Marchant (30th Infantry Division) in February 1942. (Courtesy NARA.)

Crews at Holabird Quartermaster Depot inspect a trainload of LeTourneau scrapers destined for service overseas. Holabird was a major transit station for equipment, which was loaded onto flatcars and transported to the army's Baltimore Cargo Port of Embarkation in Canton. (Courtesy LoC, FSA-OWI Collection.)

Destined for duty overseas, a column of Dodge ambulances awaits shipment at Holabird Motor Depot. They will be shipped by rail to the army's Baltimore Cargo Port of Embarkation in Canton, where Liberty and other cargo ships were loaded with munitions and supplies. The army shipped 6,865,643 tons of cargo overseas from Baltimore during the war. (Courtesy LoC, FSA-OWI Collection.)

Never before the war were high-ranking officers put through maintenance training, but the situation in 1942 was far different. With the ability to be mechanized and mobile forefront in the minds of strategists, the army recognized the need to school even generals in the science of a mechanized army. This group of officers, including a number of brigadier generals, is getting a briefing before setting out in a practice convoy. In combat, the army would only be able to move as rapidly as its supply chain could follow. (Courtesy NARA.)

Wearing a protective mask, this soldier is buffing a worn tire in preparation for a retread. With new tires scarce, Holabird took every available measure to conserve rubber. Even the rubber bits removed during the buffing process were recycled. (Courtesy LoC, FSA-OWI Collection.)

The smiling military police indicates that this photo was posed, but the warning sign was serious enough. Likely in the interest of gasoline and rubber conservation as much as for safety's sake, traffic at Holabird Quartermaster Depot was kept to a crawl. (Courtesy LoC, FSA-OWI Collection.)

Likely the most dangerous spot on the Patapsco, and located well away from the main port areas, the army's Hawkins Point Ammunition Terminal in Thom's Cove shipped armored vehicles and 1,045,062 tons of ammunition to overseas forces during the war. Two ammunition cargo ships can be seen docked at the ammunition loading pier, which could handle up to four ships at a time. Note the length of the pier, a safeguard should an accident occur while loading. The U.S. Navy also operated a magazine for the shipment of explosive ordnance at Thom's Cove. The naval magazine was originally located at Fort Carroll (best known today as the man-made island curiosity next to the Key Bridge), but moisture problems led to its relocation. Hawkins Point is the site of old Fort Armistead. (Courtesy NARA.)

The Coast Guard Yard at Curtis Bay, expanded before the war with two new shipways, a floating drydock, and numerous new buildings, was busy repairing and fitting warships of friendly nations before America's war began. This photograph, taken from a vantage point atop the *Mendota*, a new cutter under construction, shows the yard as it appeared in 1943. The *Mendota's* sister ship *Pontchartrain* is to the right. (Courtesy NARA.)

An army auxiliary vessel and numerous cargo trucks can be seen in this wartime view of Curtis Bay Coast Guard Yard. The yard was manned by 800 coastguardsmen and employed 3,600 civilians at its wartime peak. (Courtesy NARA.)

The 110-foot cutter *Manitou* (WYT-60), built at Curtis Bay and commissioned in February 1943, breaks ice in a North Atlantic fjord to open the shipping lane for convoys and their escorts. The ship was part of the Greenland Patrol, treacherous North Atlantic duty where U-boats were a constant threat. The camouflage is Thayer blue and white. *Manitou*'s sister ship, USCGC *Kaw* (WYT-61, also built at Curtis Bay) performed home-defense duties. The *Manitou* was decommissioned in 1980, the *Kaw* in 1979. (Courtesy NARA.)

The 255-foot Coast Guard cutter *Mendota* (WPG-69) is readied for launching on a rainy day at the Curtis Bay Coast Guard Yard in 1945. *Mendota* was one of six 255-foot cutters to be built during the war and one of two built at Curtis Bay (*Pontchartrain* was the second). A tarp has been placed over the platform where the launching ceremony is to take place. (Courtesy NARA.)

Dry under the tarp but dressed for an early-March Baltimore rain, Mrs. Pine, the wife of Coast Guard Academy superintendent Rear Adm. James Pine, swings the ceremonial bottle of champagne at the christening of the USCGC *Mendota* at Curtis Bay. Matrons of honor and dignitaries, including distinguished combat veteran Comdr. D. H. Dexter (in uniform), look on. (Courtesy NARA.)

Aided by a tug, the USCGC *Mendota* (WPG-69) is launched at Curtis Bay on March 1, 1945. The *Mendota* would remain at Curtis Bay for fitting out, and it would take nearly four months to transform the ship into a combat cutter. (Courtesy NARA.)

Fully equipped for combat at sea, the USCGC *Mendota* sets out into the Patapsco on June 25, 1945. The *Mendota* is carrying twin-mount 5-inch, 38-caliber dual-purpose guns fore and aft, as well as two quad 40-mm antiaircraft gun mounts. A "hedgehog" antisubmarine weapon is visible just aft of the forward 5-inch turret. The *Mendota* would provide valuable service for over 25 years. (Courtesy NARA.)

The somewhat cramped design of the 255-foot cutters spawned the rhyme, "The bow and the stern for each other yearn, and the lack of interval shows." *Pontchartrain* (WPG-70), shown here, and *Mendota* entered service just as the war was ending, seeing no combat before VJ Day. Both later saw combat service during the Vietnam War as part of Operation Market Time. They were decommissioned in 1973. (Courtesy NARA.)

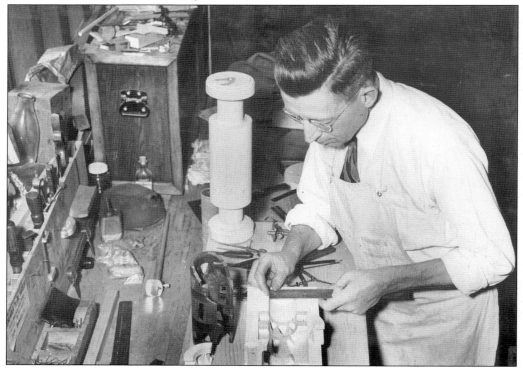

Master of a craft of days gone past, this woodworker is making precision cuts in one of the workshops at Curtis Bay Coast Guard Yard. Curtis Bay was—and is—a unique facility, heavily involved in the building and fitting of Coast Guard vessels. (Courtesy NARA.)

Fort McHenry is shown as it appeared at the beginning of the war. During the war, the hallowed inspiration for "The Star Spangled Banner"—which had famously fended off an attacking British invasion flotilla during the Battle of Baltimore in 1814—would be called upon once more to serve as an active military base. (Courtesy NARA.)

At the Coast Guard facility just outside of old Fort McHenry, coastguardsmen stand in parade formation. At Fort McHenry, coastguardsmen were trained in port security and damage control, learning skills vital in wartime but with peacetime applications as well. During the war, 23,053 trained at Fort McHenry. (Courtesy the National Park Service, Fort McHenry National Monument and Historic Shrine.)

Framed by the flag of a larger vessel, S1c. Donald Johnson, coxswain, is giving these coastguardsmen a workout in a whaleboat in the Patapsco River, just off Fort McHenry. Canton is visible in the distance. (Courtesy NARA.)

Some looking rather perplexed, these men will be required to master a variety of knots as coastguardsmen. This class is being held at the Coast Guard training facility at Fort McHenry. (Courtesy NARA.)

These coastguardsmen are in training for duty as port security officers, mastering the art of signaling at Fort McHenry under the instruction of Lt. (jg) Charles Tiemeyer. The Coast Guard patrolled ports across the country during the war, enforcing safety regulations and watching out for signs of sabotage. In Baltimore, many were assigned to guard the Hawkins Point Ammunition Terminal. (Courtesy NARA.)

From left to right, reserve officers Lt. (jg) Charles Tiemeyer and Ensigns Charles Irwin Jr., John Wilkinson, Olen Wilkens, Joseph Kelly, and Read McCaffrey, assigned to direct training activities, take time out to master the sextant and compass at Fort McHenry. From a prewar contingent of nine, the Captain of the Port would later command 60 commissioned officers and more than 1,000 enlisted men. (Courtesy NARA.)

Another kind of liberty was also highly cherished at Fort McHenry during the war—here Seaman Donald Johnson gets a liberty pass from Ens. Charles Irwin after a long day. He will probably head downtown—movies, shows, and ever-popular Fells Point, as well as the USO Club at 339 North Charles Street, were all favorite wartime diversions. (Courtesy NARA.)

Among the more popular recreational events for servicemen was boxing. Here the photographer captures a moment of excitement at the Coast Guard Barracks, Fort McHenry, as an eager crowd watches the ring. (Courtesy NARA.)

The army sponsored a series of concerts for live overseas broadcast during the spring of 1942, including this one from Fort McHenry, which was dedicated to the forces under General MacArthur in the Philippines. These broadcasts were intended to boost the morale of soldiers in the field, who at the time had yet to achieve a major victory. On March 10, MacArthur had been ordered to leave his beleaguered troops and move his headquarters to the safety of Australia. By April, his successor, Gen. Jonathan Wainwright, had retreated from the Bataan Peninsula to the fortress island of Corregidor in Manila Bay, where he surrendered to the Japanese in May.

Many American ships, including at least one aircraft carrier, were lost after combat due to a lack of damage control proficiency. The Coast Guard set out to remedy the situation. The hulk of the Liberty ship SS *Gasper de Portola* was brought alongside Fort McHenry, sunk into the mud, and used as a training vessel. Instructors would deliberately set it on fire so that coastguardsmen could practice.

Members of the 104th Observation Squadron, Maryland National Guard, service a Douglas O-46A observation aircraft at Logan Field in 1941. The 104th frequented Logan, although it was based primarily at Detrick Army Air Field near Frederick. After Pearl Harbor, the 104th performed antisubmarine patrols out of New Jersey. (Courtesy the Dundalk–Patapsco Neck Historical Society.)

This rare view shows Baltimore Municipal Airport (or Harbor Field) near the end of its service as Baltimore Army Air Base in 1945. During the war, the base served as the headquarters for the 353rd Fighter Group before it deployed to England in 1943. While no regular squadrons were based at the field, it did serve as a base for submarine-spotting patrols flown by the Civil Air Patrol. It was also a staging area for the Ferry Command, responsible for bringing new aircraft to Europe. An assortment of aircraft can be seen in this view. Below is the general layout of the airport, adapted by the author from master-plan blueprints held at the National Archives. The site of the former airport facilities is now the Dundalk Marine Terminal. (Courtesy NARA.)

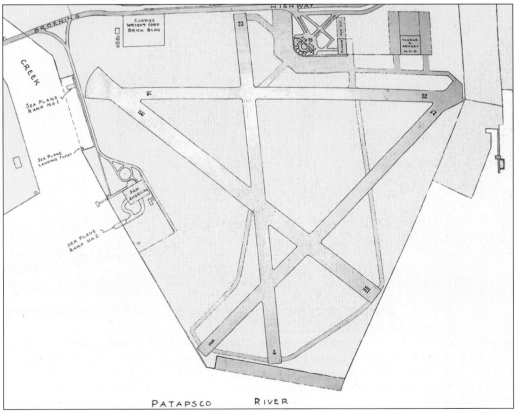

The army sent aircrews to the Martin Service Training School to train crews of the B-26 Marauder medium bomber. Personnel assigned to the navy's JM versions of the Marauder also took part in this army program. This class of Army Air Force technicians is being introduced to the nose-gear assembly of an early-model B-26. (Courtesy the Glenn L. Martin Maryland Aviation Museum.)

The B-26 featured a highly advanced electrical system. Here an attentive group of airmen in an electronics class pays close attention to the Martin instructor as he describes troubleshooting techniques. Teams will then practice on the components laid out on the table. (Courtesy the Glenn L. Martin Maryland Aviation Museum.)

Course books in hand, sailors based at Naval Air Facility Middle River stroll toward class. They are part of the Martin Mars technical training program. The navy had facilities at the Middle River factory/airstrip complex and in nearby Bengies. (Courtesy the Glenn L. Martin Maryland Aviation Museum.)

As part of the navy's training program for Mars maintenance technicians, these sailors at the Martin Service Training School are learning hands-on about the massive Wright R-3350 engine—four of which powered each of the first Martin Mars transports. (Courtesy the Glenn L. Martin Maryland Aviation Museum.)

Naval airmen and ground crews detached to the Martin-run training school for Mars pilots and mechanics line up for their first view of the plane to which they will be assigned. Redesigned from the original XPB2M, the new JRM Mars was designed from the outset as a cargo ship. Six JRMs were built, although this first aircraft would be destroyed in a crash landing shortly after this photo was taken. (Courtesy NARA.)

Glenn L. Martin Company instructors of the Martin Service Training School pose for a group photo. During the early months of the war, Martin often sent technical representatives overseas to instruct new crews in maintenance and operation. The establishment of training facilities at production plants was an improvement in efficiency and effectiveness. More than 12,000 graduated from the school during the war. (Courtesy the Glenn L. Martin Maryland Aviation Museum.)

Three

THE LIBERTY SHIPS

The SS *Patrick Henry*, first of the famous Liberty ships, shares a pier with the SS *Charles Carroll*, the second Liberty, while being fitted out in Baltimore. Both were named for founding fathers: Virginian Patrick Henry was a Revolutionary War patriot, and prominent Marylander and Declaration of Independence signatory Charles Carroll lived in Baltimore. Both ships were built at the Bethlehem-Fairfield yard. (Courtesy NARA.)

Although America had been helping to protect Atlantic convoys bound for Britain throughout 1941, German U-boats were so successful at sinking merchant ships that they were still threatening Britain's survival. Liberty ships—simple and mass-produced—provided one answer. Here the keel of the very first Liberty, the *Patrick Henry*, is being laid at the Bethlehem-Fairfield Shipyard in Baltimore on April 30, 1941. Over 2,700 would follow. (Courtesy NARA.)

Surrounded by dignitaries and thousands of curious onlookers, the SS *Patrick Henry* is shown prepared for launch on September 27, 1941. Rear Adm. Emory Land, head of the Maritime Commission, gave the keynote speech, while Vice Pres. Henry Wallace's wife, Ilo, christened the vessel. The Bethlehem-Fairfield yard had been built specifically for production of the new Liberty ships, and it would produce about one-sixth of the total built. (Courtesy NARA.)

While the Baltimore Civic Band played the "Star Spangled Banner," the SS *Patrick Henry* slid into the Patapsco River and into the history books on September 27, 1941. *Patrick Henry* was one of 14 merchant ships launched on "Liberty Fleet Day," an occasion for a special radio address by President Roosevelt. Quickly fitted out, she was commissioned on December 30, just weeks after the Pearl Harbor attack. (Courtesy NARA.)

The SS *Patrick Henry* is seen after being launched, fitted out, and armed. Note the old 5-inch, 31-caliber gun in place on the aft deck and the gun tubs for smaller-caliber antiaircraft weapons. Crewed by Merchant Marines with a complement of U.S. Naval Armed Guard sailors, Liberty ships saw extensive and dangerous action during the war, carrying vital cargo, and around 200 were lost due to enemy action. (Courtesy NARA.)

Her fitting-out complete, the SS *Patrick Henry* leaves Baltimore Harbor for duty in the Atlantic. She is wearing a standard early-war dark grey paint scheme. The *Patrick Henry* served throughout the war in Atlantic convoys, finally being scrapped at the same place she was constructed, the Bethlehem-Fairfield yard, in 1958. One Liberty built at Fairfield, the SS *John W. Brown*, survives as a museum ship in Baltimore and is open to visitors. The *Brown* is the only Fairfield-built Liberty, and one of only two total, to be preserved. The other is California-built SS *Jeremiah O'Brien*, docked in San Francisco. (Courtesy NARA.)

The majority of Bethlehem-Fairfield's shipbuilders had never worked on a ship before coming to the plant. Nevertheless, the company was able to train a skilled workforce and was a fierce competitor with other East Coast yards—oftentimes leading all of them in efficiency. These workers are in a construction class. (Courtesy LoC, FSA-OWI Collection.)

A key architect of the Liberty ship program, industrial magnate Henry J. Kaiser successfully applied assembly line techniques to shipbuilding. The Liberty ships' large degree of standardization and their subcomponent construction sped building time. Here, two workers study blueprints to make sure subcomponents are correctly placed. (Courtesy LoC, FSA-OWI Collection.)

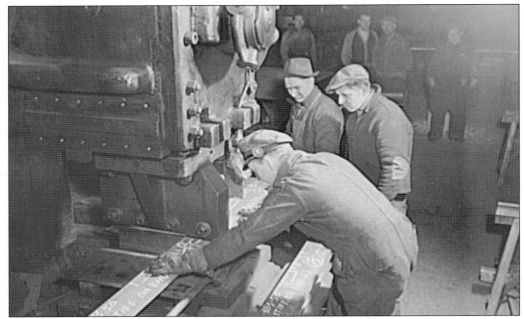

These metalworkers at the Pullman-Standard Car Company in Curtis Bay are fabricating components for Liberty ships to be built at Bethlehem-Fairfield. All major subassemblies for the Liberties, including boilers and engines from out of state, were transported into the yard by rail. This plant, leased by Bethlehem Steel, was located just a few miles from the Fairfield yard. (Courtesy LoC, FSA-OWI Collection.)

Liberty ships were of virtually all-welded construction, making welding one of the most sought-after professions at Fairfield and other shipyards. Workers came from across America to work at Bethlehem-Fairfield. These welders at the Pullman-Standard Car plant are working on structural subcomponents that will be transported by rail to the main yard. (Courtesy LoC, FSA-OWI Collection.)

These welders at the Pullman-Standard Car plant are welding a pipe fitting to a large sheet steel section. Chalk notes on the steel give measurements and other information. (Courtesy LoC, FSA-OWI Collection.)

Steel bulkhead sections are placed on rail cars for the journey from Curtis Bay to the Fairfield yard. Old locomotives were reconditioned to work the route. These and other components would find their way to a 40-acre holding yard but would not wait there for long. At one point during the war, Fairfield was launching a Liberty ship every 35 hours! (Courtesy LoC, FSA-OWI Collection.)

This worker is laying keel blocks, evenly spaced every four feet, upon which the keel will be laid. This had to be precise, as the blocks would hold the weight of the heavy keel and would help support it as additional hull plates were welded. (Courtesy LoC, FSA-OWI Collection.)

Standing on platforms, workmen guide parts of a flat keel into place, one of the first steps in building a massive ship such as a Liberty. Within mere days, the workers will require use of the permanent scaffolding in the background as the vessel fills the shipway. Some Liberty ships were completed and delivered within a matter of weeks from the laying of their keels. (Courtesy NARA.)

Looking northwest along the shipways, this view captures the massive cranes at Fairfield. The closest crane was an older, fixed type that arched over two shipways. These cranes would be needed to lift massive ship components in holding areas behind each way. (Courtesy LoC, FSA-OWI Collection.)

The bow of this Liberty ship is about to be joined as the sun starts to set. The sign on Number 3 Way reads, "Defense Plant: Part of the Arsenal of Democracy," although the workers in this vital industry probably did not need a reminder. (Courtesy LoC, FSA-OWI Collection.)

This Liberty ship is nearly complete, and as dusk sets in, the floodlights have been turned on to aid the night shift. At lower right, you can see the tracks upon which the rolling cranes sat, enabling them to move up and down the shipways and holding stations. (Courtesy LoC, FSA-OWI Collection.)

Work on the essential Liberty ships could not be allowed to cease with the coming of darkness. Here the Bethlehem-Fairfield Shipyard is shown floodlit after dusk with the night shift hard at work. Subassemblies and large steel sections are stacked in the foreground. The Fairfield yard was one of the entities granted an exemption from compulsory blackout drills. (Courtesy NARA.)

This welder is working through the night on large sections being welded in the Fairfield yard. The shipways are in the background. (Courtesy LoC, FSA-OWI Collection.)

A team of welders is shown constructing the shaft through which the propeller will mount. Though hurriedly put together, Liberty ships were still complex machines operated in some of the world's harshest environments. Work such as this needed to be precise. (Courtesy NARA.)

The massive screws for Liberty ships under construction dwarf shipyard workers in this picture, taken at Bethlehem-Fairfield in May 1943. Having attached the shaft to the propeller, these workers are beginning to hoist the assembly for installation in the SS *Frederick Douglass*. Many of these screws were produced by the Bartlett-Hayward Division of Koppers Company in Baltimore. Bartlett-Hayward won the Army-Navy "E" Award with five stars and at one point was able to produce two of these propellers each day. Liberty ships each had one propeller, driven by easy-to-operate triple-expansion steam engines. (Courtesy NARA.)

The SS *William Pepper* is decked out for launching, with patriotic bunting around the shipway offices. It seems as if everyone stopped work to watch the event. Bethlehem-Fairfield launched 384 Liberty ships, plus an additional 94 Victory ships (the larger, faster follow-on to the Liberty). (Courtesy LoC, FSA-OWI Collection.)

Onlookers marvel as a gigantic Liberty slides past them, off the way and into the Patapsco. The ships were a common sight from shore, as each one was run through various tests before delivery. (Courtesy LoC, FSA-OWI Collection.)

In 1942, work on the Liberty ships at Fairfield was interrupted by an urgent requirement for landing ships for the Allied invasion of Sicily. Here LST-401, one of the 30 Fairfield-built LSTs (Landing Ship, Tank), is launched with workmen waving from the bow on October 16, 1942. The Fairfield-built LSTs were all transferred to the British Royal Navy before the invasion; seven were lost during the war. (Courtesy NARA.)

The SS *Richard Henry Lee* and SS *John Randolph*, with another Liberty in the rear, are shown fitting out at one of Fairfield's fitting piers. Later, when work began on the Victory ships, two of Fairfield's ways were replaced with additional fitting piers. (Courtesy LoC, FSA-OWI Collection.)

Chipper Albert Townes and his apprentice, Robert Cowan, work on the deckhouse of the SS *Frederick Douglass*. At the time the *Frederick Douglass* was built, over 6,000 African Americans were at work in the Bethlehem-Fairfield yard, many in skilled positions. It was perhaps a fitting tribute to the great abolitionist, but many wartime gains would need to be fought for again after the war. (Courtesy NARA.)

Thelma Holmes was the first female welder ever hired by the Bethlehem-Fairfield Shipyard, and she was later promoted to welding instructor in the training department. She is wearing her instructor's badge. Proving that women could do a "man's job" just as well as any man helped open the door for dramatic social changes and new opportunities for women in the decades after the war. (Courtesy NARA.)

An arc welder at the Bethlehem-Fairfield Shipyard takes a brief respite to smile for the Office of War Information photographer. As the traditional workforce went off to war, and with Baltimore already short on war labor, women and minorities became increasingly important in fields where access had been denied to them before the war. (Courtesy NARA.)

This patriotic poster, put out by the navy, encouraged shipyard workers to stay productive. Napping and sluggishness were, of course, discouraged. Coming out of the Depression, there was no shortage of eager employees to fill vital positions; Fairfield interviewed as many as 2,300 applicants each day!

Smiling as they flash the victory "V," welders S. L. Ramsey (left) and Benny Chan pause during construction of the Liberty ship SS *Frederick Douglass* at the Bethlehem-Fairfield Shipyard in May 1943. One of several Liberty ships to be named for prominent African Americans, the *Frederick Douglass* was named after the famed abolitionist author and orator who had spent much of his childhood as a slave in Baltimore. (Courtesy NARA.)

It is "Rosie the Riveter" that often defines the historical image of women during the war, but "Rosie the Welder" was there, too! Taking a moment to pose for the photographer, this welder at the Fairfield yard looks set to handle anything. Though many would return to traditional roles after the war, others would never again desire to fit the "housewife" mold. (Courtesy LoC, FSA-OWI Collection.)

Photographer Arthur Siegel captured this image of shipyard workers breaking for lunch at Fairfield. Work on the Liberty ships went on seven days a week, and 12-hour shifts were common. Lunch was a most welcome time to relax. (Courtesy LoC, FSA-OWI Collection.)

This group of shipbuilders at Bethlehem-Fairfield seems to embody a sense of wartime determination. The man at right wears a victory "V" on his hard hat. Several photographers working for the Office of War Information, including Howard Liberman, who took this photo, made trips to Fairfield to capture the Liberty shipbuilders in action. (Courtesy LoC, FSA-OWI Collection.)

These two workers are catching up on the latest war news, reading headline coverage of the Pacific Campaign in the *Baltimore Sun*. By the late spring of 1943, when this photograph was taken, the headlines out of the Pacific were mostly positive, the Allies having put Japan on the defensive. (Courtesy LoC, FSA-OWI Collection.)

Welding gear, flaming torches, hot steel, and the Baltimore summer sun made for an uncomfortable workday. This welder has found one way to cool off, enjoying a cup of ice cream on his lunchtime break. (Courtesy LoC, FSA-OWI Collection.)

This detailed overview of the Bethlehem-Fairfield yard was taken by a U.S. Navy aircrew in 1945, by which time the ways had been widened and reduced to 14 in order to accommodate the new Victory ships, seen under construction. The large cranes and the massive subcomponent holding areas are clearly visible. Larger and faster than the Liberty ships, Victory ships retained many of the production features that had enabled mass-production of their smaller predecessors. Fairfield built 94 Victory ships before war's end, a number of them being converted to U.S. Navy use at the Key Highway yard. The first, SS *Frederick Victory*, was launched on September 9, 1944. Today the entrance to the Harbor Tunnel runs straight through the site of the massive Fairfield complex, little trace of which remains. (Courtesy NARA.)

Fire was a constant hazard at the shipyards, and it was up to firemen like these men of the Bethlehem-Fairfield Fire Patrol to respond to any emergency. Some fire crews were even given instruction in shipyard safety at the Coast Guard's training facility at Fort McHenry. (Courtesy LoC, FSA-OWI Collection.)

No doubt happy to be headed home after a long day, these Bethlehem-Fairfield workers smile for Marjory Collins aboard the ferry from Fairfield to Curtis Bay. The Wilson Line operated two 2,500-seat steamers under contract to the Maritime Commission, charging 5¢ each way from Curtis Bay or Broadway Pier to Fairfield. (Courtesy LoC, FSA-OWI Collection.)

Four

BALTIMORE'S AVIATION INDUSTRY

A cheerful-looking President Roosevelt shakes hands with Glenn Martin during an official visit to the Middle River plant in this wartime publicity photo. Glenn Martin had been an aviation pioneer, following closely in the footsteps of the Wright brothers, Glenn Curtiss, and other early airplane designers. He had completed and flown his first airplane in 1909; 20 years later, he moved his growing company to Baltimore. (Courtesy NARA.)

At the Glenn L. Martin Company's Middle River facility, rows of Martin Model 167 aircraft components await assembly. This factory building was financed by France, which was eager to purchase the advanced 167 as a defense against German aggression. Despite its modern air force, France fell to the Germans in 1940. (Courtesy the Glenn L. Martin Maryland Aviation Museum.)

These men are working on a Martin Model 167, later called the Maryland in British service. These advanced attack aircraft were initially ordered by France and saw service against the Germans in 1940. Later, they were used by both Vichy French forces and their British opponents in North Africa and the Mediterranean. (Courtesy the Glenn L. Martin Maryland Aviation Museum.)

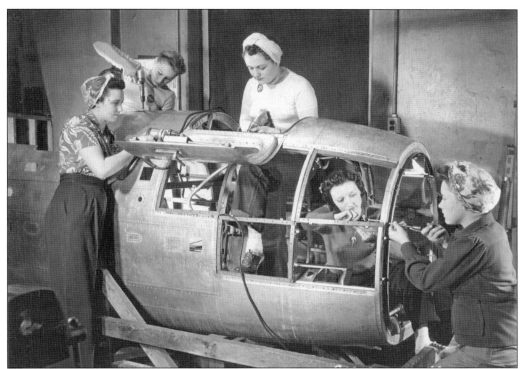

This crew of women workers, some of the first to be hired by the Glenn L. Martin Company, work on the framed-glass nose section of a Maryland bomber destined for service with the British Royal Air Force. Four hundred ninety-six of the type were built, including over 200 delivered to France before its fall. (Courtesy the Glenn L. Martin Maryland Aviation Museum.)

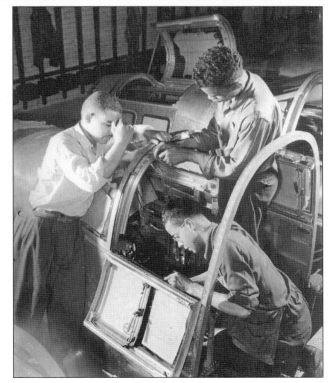

These men at the Glenn L. Martin plant in Canton are working on the cockpit of a Maryland bomber destined for Allied service. Major subcomponents such as the cockpit/nose assembly, wings, and fuselage sections were built at Canton, then shipped to Middle River for final assembly. Aircraft produced by Martin had a reputation for being highly advanced and saw service in most theaters of war. (Courtesy NARA.)

At the Glenn L. Martin plant in Canton, a worker is maneuvering a Maryland bomber's wing section into place using an overhead pulley. Canton, where Martin leased facilities from the Canton Company, was the site of the first Glenn L. Martin factory in Baltimore. (Courtesy the Glenn L. Martin Maryland Aviation Museum.)

This Royal Air Force Maryland is off on a sortie from a British-held desert airstrip in North Africa. The Maryland and Baltimore bombers, produced in quantity for Britain, saw extensive service in North Africa and the Mediterranean. (Courtesy the Glenn L. Martin Maryland Aviation Museum.)

Floridian Kathryn Johnson joined the Glenn L. Martin Company in 1942 as a spotwelder. She promptly set the spotwelding record (46,000) while working a night shift. Many workers from distant states flocked to the Baltimore area during the war; many took high-skill jobs in the aircraft and shipbuilding industries. Here Ms. Johnson is shown working on cowl flaps for a PBM-3 Mariner. (Courtesy NARA.)

Spaghetti-like aluminum tubing destined for installation in a massive PBM Mariner seems to engulf this young war worker in the Glenn L. Martin plant in Middle River. (Courtesy NARA.)

Before delivery to the navy, each seaplane's hull was tested for watertightness by pumping water into the plane and checking for leaks on the outside. Here a team is using a flashlight to carefully inspect each rivet and seam. Seaplane construction was a combination of the arts of boat building and aircraft manufacture. (Courtesy NARA.)

The Glenn L. Martin Company built not only aircraft, but the gun turrets that provided their defensive armament as well. Martin was the first company to develop an electric gun turret, first used on the B-26. Here, Martin electric gun turrets are being checked out before installation in PBM Mariner aircraft, one of the last steps in final assembly. (Courtesy NARA.)

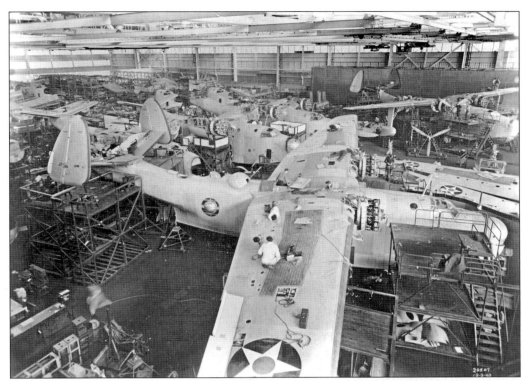

Wearing pre–Battle of Midway national insignia, a crop of new PBM-1 Mariners take shape at the Glenn L. Martin plant, giving some indication of the size of the facility—just one building at the sprawling Middle River site! Close to 7,000 military aircraft were built at Middle River during the war. (Courtesy NARA.)

This well-dressed Martin employee, working in the forward gun turret mount of a PBM Mariner, gives some sense of the massive seaplane's size. Glenn Martin loved the idea of extremely large flying boats, and his next creation—the Martin Mars—would dwarf even this huge PBM. (Courtesy NARA.)

A nearly-complete PBM Mariner leaves the hangar on a sunny day. The gun turrets have yet to be installed. The Mariner was used for a variety of missions, including transport, antisubmarine warfare, and nighttime anti-shipping interdiction. (Courtesy NARA.)

Far away from its Baltimore birthplace, a Martin PBM Mariner displays its breathtaking short-takeoff ability "somewhere in the Pacific." This dramatic takeoff was accomplished with the use of JATO (Jet Assisted Take-Off) rockets affixed to the sides of the plane. The Mariner saw extensive service with a number of navies during the war and, with a production run of 1,366, was Martin's most-produced navy airplane. (Courtesy NARA.)

Rows of gleaming B-26 Marauders crowd the floor of Plant 2 at Glenn L. Martin's Middle River complex. The Marauder was truly state of the art when it made its debut in 1941, the latest in a long line of advanced bomber aircraft developed by Martin. After Pearl Harbor, they were quickly rushed into combat, and they established a solid record against Japanese forces. (Courtesy the Glenn L. Martin Maryland Aviation Museum.)

Two Martin employees shake hands and celebrate their handiwork's victory over Japanese forces in the Aleutians. B-26 Marauders were credited with sinking a Japanese cruiser with torpedoes (Marauders were the only U.S. Army aircraft so equipped). (Courtesy the Glenn L. Martin Maryland Aviation Museum.)

A line of fresh early-model B-26s line the ramp at Middle River. The early B-26 was prone to accidents at the hands of novice pilots, a fact attributed by some observers to the aircraft's slender wings. Critics called the plane "the Baltimore Whore," as it had "no visible means of support." Yet in combat, early B-26s such as these acquitted themselves well and were very popular with the crews that flew them. They were among the first aircraft sent to the Pacific after Pearl Harbor and served with distinction in the South Pacific, Southwest Pacific, and Alaskan theaters. In Europe, later Marauders boasted the lowest loss rate of any bomber aircraft. Just beyond the Marauders in this photo is a line of P-40 Warhawks of the 59th Pursuit Squadron, assigned to the air defense of Baltimore during the opening months of the war. (Courtesy the Glenn L. Martin Maryland Aviation Museum.)

Posing in front of B-26 Marauder No. 390, this group of Martin employees proudly displays the "V for Victory" sign popularized by Winston Churchill. There were 5,266 Marauders of all types produced, more than any other Martin airplane. (Courtesy the Glenn L. Martin Maryland Aviation Museum.)

These men are working in the nose section of a B-26 medium bomber. The sign on the side of the plane is intended to encourage efficient work, reading, "I'm one of the world's hottest Bombers—Get me out of here by 10-13 so I can start puttin' the heat on the axis." (Courtesy the Glenn L. Martin Maryland Aviation Museum.)

This test pilot is receiving his final instructions and preparing to take a new B-26 on its maiden flight. The test pilots kept civil defense lookouts on Kent Island on their toes—lookouts were required to note the arrival of every aircraft and were right under the Martin test-flight pattern! (Courtesy the Glenn L. Martin Maryland Aviation Museum.)

A group of Martin Company and Army Air Force ferry pilots relax in the control tower at Middle River. As a ferry terminal, Baltimore was a departure point for crews flying aircraft north to Newfoundland and across the Atlantic to depots in Ireland. From Ireland, the aircraft would be flown out to operational units as replacements. (Courtesy the Glenn L. Martin Maryland Aviation Museum.)

Martin employees examine autographs on B-26B *Mild and Bitter* (452 Bomber Squadron/322 Bomb Group), the first Marauder to fly 100 combat missions. (B-26B *Flak Bait*, now at the National Air and Space Museum, flew a record 202 combat missions.) Sent back to America for a publicity tour, the plane was autographed by hundreds of servicemen from the 322nd Bomb Group's base in England. (Courtesy the Glenn L. Martin Maryland Aviation Museum.)

The 322nd Bomb Group flew some extremely dangerous and costly missions in their B-26s, including a 10-plane raid on Holland in which not a single plane returned. Both *Mild and Bitter* and *Flak Bait* were veteran aircraft of the unit. *Mild and Bitter* took 166 airmen into combat, 26 of whom earned medals, and though hit numerous times, never suffered a casualty. (Courtesy the Glenn L. Martin Maryland Aviation Museum.)

At the National Defense Vocational Training School for Colored, School No. 453 (775 Waesche Street), Col. A. Robert Ginsburgh (second from right) gets a demonstration of sheet-metal drilling from Clyde Millen. Mr. Millen had already been offered a position by the Glenn L. Martin Company. It took prodding, but the Martin Company became one of the first to offer skilled positions to African Americans. (Courtesy NARA.)

At National Defense Vocational Training School No. 250 on East Baltimore Street, army Lt. Joseph Genovese examines the work of student George Adam from Massachusetts. Many of these students were assured of jobs at the Glenn L. Martin plant upon graduation as skilled sheet-metal workers, and Adam, who could not hear or speak, had already received an offer. For many, the war brought unprecedented opportunities. (Courtesy NARA.)

Glenn L. Martin employees are shown attaching aluminum skin to wing sections for the Baltimore bombers taking shape in the background. The Canton plant—site of the first Martin factory in Baltimore—was nowhere near as glamorous as the Middle River facilities but manufactured many of the more complex components of the Baltimore bomber. Martin built 1,575 Baltimores. (Courtesy NARA.)

At the Glenn L. Martin plant in Canton, two workers assemble the Plexiglas-type plastic nose of a Baltimore bomber. The all-plastic clear-vision nose was pioneered by Martin on the B-26 and became standard for bombardier stations on most World War II–era aircraft. (Courtesy NARA.)

While Baltimore remained a segregated city until well after the war, the war did break a few workplace barriers, at least temporarily. Here workers in the Glenn L. Martin plant in Canton work on landing gear for the Baltimore bomber. Unlike Eastern Aircraft on Broening Highway, where the main assembly areas were integrated, no skilled African Americans worked at Martin's main plants during the war. (Courtesy NARA.)

This Martin Baltimore bomber, built at Canton and Middle River, has lost part of its vertical stabilizer to flak in the Mediterranean theater. The plane is serving with the Royal Air Force, which was the primary operator of the type. Few wartime photographs exist of the Baltimore and its predecessor, the Maryland. (Courtesy the Glenn L. Martin Maryland Aviation Museum.)

The Martin XPB2M-1 Mars, at 70 tons and with a wingspan of 200 feet, was the largest aircraft in the world at the time it was built. Here Martin employees involved in the project pose with the massive flying boat in front of one of the camouflaged hangars. Although technically a prototype, the Mars saw considerable wartime service hauling cargo to the Pacific theater. (Courtesy NARA.)

Originally conceived as a flying battleship, the prototype XPB2M Mars hauled massive loads of cargo to the Pacific theater as part of the Naval Air Transport Service. Shown here in Middle River sporting early-war navy camouflage of blue-grey over light grey, the Mars is about to embark on a 32-hour endurance test flight on October 9, 1943. (Courtesy NARA.)

The first production JRM-1, *Hawaii Mars*, is launched stern first, ship-style, at Strawberry Point on Middle River. Henry Kaiser had even proposed building the planes in massive quantities as flying Liberty ships. Glenn Martin was not keen on sharing his design with another manufacturer, and Kaiser turned to Howard Hughes to build giant flying boats—a far less successful venture! (Courtesy NARA.)

Testing new aircraft always carries an element of danger. The sad end to the first JRM, *Hawaii Mars*, came near the end of the war, on August 5, 1945, in a hard landing on the Chesapeake. Fortunately the accident was not fatal, and all but one of the occupants walked away more or less unscathed. The plane was a total loss. (Courtesy NARA.)

A Baltimore salvage crew raises the mangled tail section of the *Hawaii Mars* from the Chesapeake Bay, just hours after the crash. Divers attached lines to the sunken portions of the plane. The name *Hawaii Mars* was later given to the last JRM built. Of the five remaining JRMs, two—the second *Hawaii Mars* and *Philippine Mars*—are still in service in 2005 as fire tankers! (Courtesy NARA.)

Uninterrupted by an icy Baltimore evening, these second-shift workers on platforms dripping with icicles attend to the Curtiss Electric propeller of a B-26. (Courtesy the Glenn L. Martin Maryland Aviation Museum.)

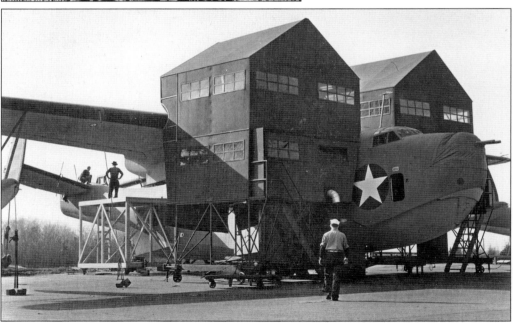

February in Maryland can be brutally cold, as any Baltimorean will likely agree, and this contraption was devised to make work a bit more comfortable for crews working on PBM engines at the Martin plant in Middle River. Each insulating "house" is two stories tall. (Courtesy NARA.)

Workers are pictured at the Glenn L. Martin plant in Middle River during a change in shift. The camouflage applied to the factory is quite apparent. While enemy bombers never appeared in the skies over Baltimore to test its concealment properties, the paint did succeed in blocking ventilation during the hot and humid summers, causing widespread employee discomfort. (Courtesy the Glenn L. Martin Maryland Aviation Museum.)

The impact of having so many men involved in military service touched almost every profession. With military police regulars needed in every theater of war, auxiliaries such as Madeline Lippe of New York stepped in to fill vital security positions. Ms. Lippe trained in law enforcement—and learned jujitsu—before being accepted as an MP. (Courtesy NARA.)

This part-Baltimore-built Eastern Aircraft TBM Avenger from the USS *Monterey* (CVL-26) is shown en route to Guam in July 1944. General Motors' outstanding performance in building these aircraft, which it did with almost no assistance from established aircraft manufacturers, is considered a case study in effective conversion from civilian to military manufacture during the war. The Baltimore plant received the Army-Navy "E" Award with one star. (Courtesy NARA.)

After the TBF Avenger's dramatic debut during the Battle of Midway, production of Grumman's famous torpedo bombers was shifted to an untested entity in airplane construction—General Motors—in order to free Grumman to build F6F Hellcat fighters. GM created a whole new division, Eastern Aircraft, and split production of the Avenger (as the TBM) among three plants: the Broening Highway plant in Baltimore; Tarrytown, New York; and Trenton, New Jersey. The General Motors plant on Broening Highway was actually two facilities in one: the left third of the building, where Eastern Aircraft operated, was part of the Fisher Body Division, while the right two-thirds were operated by Chevrolet. Early in the war, the Chevrolet plant was still producing trucks for the army. Eastern Aircraft later expanded into part of the Chevrolet complex. Note the shrubbery Chevrolet logo at lower right. (Courtesy NARA.)

Eastern Aircraft in Baltimore fabricated ailerons and the aft fuselage section of the Avenger, then shipped the parts north to Trenton. There the Baltimore aft section, Tarrytown wings and nose, and Trenton midsection were assembled into a complete airplane. Here an aviation machinist's mate aboard the USS *Hornet* (CV-12) poses proudly alongside the Baltimore-built "stinger" end of one of his squadron's TBMs in June 1944. (Courtesy NARA.)

Many naval aviators flew the Avenger, widely regarded as the finest torpedo bomber of the war, but none achieved the fame of Lt. (jg) George H. W. Bush of the USS *San Jacinto* (CVL-30), later the 41st president of the United States. Bush's service as an Avenger pilot figured prominently in his life, both public and private. Lieutenant Bush is shown in the cockpit of his Baltimore/Tarrytown/Trenton-built TBM. (Courtesy the George Bush Presidential Library.)

Five

WORKING FOR VICTORY

Using a Towson-built Friez weather device to measure wind direction and speed, the weather technician on the right makes a final check before clearing a flight from a military airfield in late 1944. With forces in just about every conceivable climatic condition during the war, instruments such as this were vital. Friez won the Army-Navy "E" Award with three stars during the war. (Courtesy NARA.)

For the men of the Merchant Marine, Navy, and Coast Guard on duty in the Atlantic, the war was already on when this photo was taken in August 1941. American vessels with large "neutrality flags" painted on their sides are shown fitting out at the Bethlehem-Baltimore shipyard on Key Highway. The large Stars and Stripes were intended to announce the neutrality of the vessel and thus ward off attack. A number of American ships were attacked, and seven were sunk by Germany between May 1941 and the Pearl Harbor attack, including a U.S. Navy destroyer—the USS *Reuben James*—which was lost in October 1941. The Key Highway yard was busy repairing battle-damaged foreign vessels, victims of U-boats during the trans-Atlantic crossing, as early as 1940. (Courtesy NARA.)

The newly completed USS *Vinton*, a North Carolina–built Victory ship destined for U.S. Navy service, arrives off of Hawkins Point in September 1944. Clean and freshly painted, the *Vinton* looks like anything but a combat vessel. The vessel is shown headed for the Bethlehem-Baltimore shipyard, where it will be converted to an attack cargo ship, or "AKA." (Courtesy NARA.)

This Victory ship means business! With a new coat of sea blue camouflage, the USS *Vinton* (AKA-83) is shown after a thorough working-over at the Bethlehem-Baltimore yard. As fitted, *Vinton* could carry 15 LCVPs and 8 LCM-3s (Landing Craft, Medium). Assisted by the tugboat *Porter* of the Curtis Bay Towing Company, the *Vinton* would soon depart for the invasion of Okinawa. (Courtesy NARA.)

Bethlehem's Key Highway yard, also known as Bethlehem-Baltimore, was engaged in the repair and militarization of ships during the war. One of its specialties was the repair of battle-damaged merchant ships, including one Norwegian vessel estimated as being two-thirds destroyed upon arrival! Other merchant ships were armed for protection or completely converted for military use. Federal Hill is in the background at upper right. (Courtesy NARA.)

Maryland Drydock Company was also a busy place during the war. Like the Key Highway yard, it took on repair and outfitting work for military and civilian vessels, handling over 3,300 ships during the war years. After the war, the company demilitarized ships for commercial use. Maryland Drydock was located in Fairfield alongside the Bethlehem yard, part of which is visible on the left. (Courtesy NARA.)

A load of scrapped automobiles, including a Ford coupe, makes its way to the United Iron and Metal Company for recycling in a trailer that looks ready to burst. United Iron and Metal had its main operation at Catherine Street and Wilkens Avenue and a satellite facility off Pulaski Highway. Compacted scrap went mainly to Bethlehem Steel in Sparrows Point. A majority of United's employees were African American. (Courtesy LoC, FSA-OWI Collection.)

In a Baltimore yard, most likely United Iron and Metal Company, this crane operator is handling steel scrap that will be melted down and put to wartime use. As part of the government's wartime conservation program, the public was urged to contribute steel scraps, keeping a flow of recycled steel available for more vital purposes. (Courtesy NARA.)

An automobile no longer, this scrapped vehicle has been compacted for shipment and melting using the large baling press of a Baltimore scrapyard. Another car waits its turn in the background. The squashed cars will be sent to steel mills for recycling and reuse in vital war machinery. (Courtesy NARA.)

Steel products were vital to the war effort, and the Bethlehem Steel works in Sparrows Point contributed its share. This engineer is shown in his narrow-gauge locomotive, used to haul ingots at the plant, in May 1942. The Sparrows Point plant produced 19,460,628 net tons of steel during the war. (Courtesy NARA.)

Careful to watch his thickly gloved hands, this worker at the Bethlehem Steel plant at Sparrows Point is drawing wire from steel strips in May 1942. Sparrows Point received the bulk of all scrap steel collected in Maryland and promptly recycled it into wartime products. (Courtesy NARA.)

At age 60, courier Fred Heeben of Bethlehem Steel in Sparrows Point was still going strong in May 1942. He is shown with a handful of time cards for delivery during a war production drive, his bicycle coming in handy at the massive steel complex, the second-largest in the United States at the time. (Courtesy NARA.)

Bethlehem Steel operated both its massive steel mill and a shipbuilding complex at Sparrows Point during the war. The shipyard, shown here, approximately doubled in size at war's outset and constructed a variety of ship types for the U.S. Navy and commercial concerns. The 98 wartime ships launched at Sparrows Point were built more traditionally than their welded Liberty and Victory brethren at Fairfield. (Courtesy NARA.)

In October 1941, during a tour of federally funded national defense vocational training schools in the city, army Lt. B. Powell Harrison is addressing a group at Patterson Park High School. Recognizing that it was in the nation's interest to begin preparations for war, the government hastened to offer training for workers in key defense industries, particularly aircraft manufacture and other highly skilled work. (Courtesy NARA.)

Assistant foreman Joseph Witte operates a lathe at the White Engineering Company, fabricating parts of turbo-supercharger components for aircraft engines. He is one of the many "disabled" war workers who helped redefine perceptions of persons with disabilities during the war. (Courtesy LoC, FSA-OWI Collection.)

With newcomers flooding into the city to take wartime jobs, three wartime work shifts, and automobile drivers kept off the streets by rationing, the wear and tear on the Baltimore Transit Company's vehicles was enormous. Here, likely in the firm's Carroll Park Shops, a row of buses awaits heavy maintenance. On a given day, repairmen could face well over 150 out-of-service mass transit vehicles. (Courtesy LoC, FSA-OWI Collection.)

The Baltimore Transit Company did not get many new vehicles during the war, so mechanics such as this cheerful fellow were responsible for keeping old and weary machines running. Prewar buses were constantly overhauled, while decommissioned trolleys dating back to World War I were refurbished and pressed into service. Baltimore Transit served between 3.3 and 3.9 million commuters annually during the war. (Courtesy LoC, FSA-OWI Collection.)

Men and a small number of women served as bus drivers and trolley conductors during the war. These three are having a laugh over coffee at the Baltimore Transit Company's canteen. Baltimore Transit Company employed well over 3,500 people at its wartime peak. (Courtesy LoC, FSA-OWI Collection.)

Revere Copper and Brass, founded in 1801 by Paul Revere in Boston, had a major operation in Baltimore established in 1928. Among the many items produced at its plants were metal discs for ammunition casings. Revere employed nearly 2,400 people at the time this photo was taken in February 1944, and it won the Army-Navy "E" Award with four stars. (Courtesy NARA.)

Here blood is being checked and packed in crates for shipment by workers of the Baltimore Red Cross, which sent 323,941 pints of blood to the armed forces during the war. The Baltimore Red Cross, which included Baltimore and Howard Counties, also raised $10,573,389 in war fund contributions. (Courtesy the Glenn L. Martin Maryland Aviation Museum.)

During the war, the family-owned Owens Yacht Company in Dundalk manufactured 2,150 landing craft—one of the most necessary and heralded weapons in a war that relied heavily on amphibious invasion, and singled out by General Eisenhower as one of the most critical items that made victory possible. Here a completed LCVP (Landing Craft, Vehicles and Personnel) is swung toward a freight car for transport. (Courtesy NARA.)

Popularly referred to as the "Higgins Boat" after its designer, New Orleans boat builder Andrew Higgins, the LCVP saw extensive service during the war. It is perhaps best remembered as the workhorse of the Normandy D-Day invasion in June 1944, though it participated in every major amphibious invasion from 1943 onward. Flat-bottomed with a shallow draft, and with an efficient front ramp for disembarkation, it could get close to shore and quickly deposit men and materiel on a landing beach. Not comfortable, and hardly safe as they made their way toward heavily defended shores, they were nonetheless indispensable to the war effort. Here workers at the Owens Yacht Company are shown building the boats in assembly-line fashion. (Courtesy NARA.)

A number of Baltimore scientists were awarded the President's Certificate of Merit for outstanding war work. In a post-war ceremony at Johns Hopkins University, awards are being presented by Col. Arthur Shreve (first row, second from right) of the Maryland Military District. These recipients are (first row, from left to right) Prof. Joyce Alvin Bearden of Johns Hopkins University, Dr. Harry Eagle of the National Institutes of Health, Dr. W. Mansfield Clark of Johns Hopkins, Dr. George Washington Corner of the Carnegie Institution of Washington, Dr. Louise Kelley of Goucher College, and Dr. Edwin Cowles Andrus of Johns Hopkins (immediately behind Dr. Kelley). (Courtesy NARA.)

Six

TO WAR

OWI photographer Jack Delano captured this image of Coast Guard honor guards offering a 21-gun salute at the funeral of Merchant Marine Herman Sweitzer of Baltimore. Killed in a collision between a tanker and an ammunition freighter off Norfolk, Virginia, Sweitzer was the first Merchant Marine to be honored with a military funeral. In the Battle of the Atlantic, the distinction between civilian and combatant was nearly nonexistent.

Albert Frantum of Baltimore mans a three-inch gun aboard an unnamed Coast Guard combat cutter in the North Atlantic. Coastguardsmen served in many different combat roles and were heavily involved in the fight against Nazi U-boats in the Battle of the Atlantic. Many trained at Curtis Bay, while others attended the Coast Guard's school for damage control at Fort McHenry. (Courtesy NARA.)

In transit back to the United States, PFC George Shriner Jr., of Washington Boulevard, stands by his temporary home away from home at Pearl Harbor, Hawaii, in 1945. He served as a radar operator with the 6th Marine Defense Battalion on Midway. (Courtesy George Shriner Jr. via David Shriner.)

Baltimoreans Lt. Sarah Pattillo (left) and Lt. May Lewis decorate the 42nd General Hospital Christmas tree in 1942. The University of Maryland–Baltimore School of Medicine–affiliated 42nd was based in Brisbane, Australia. The school-affiliated general hospital units (the 18th and 118th from Johns Hopkins and the 42nd and 142nd from University of Maryland) had local medical personnel from the schools as their core. (Courtesy NARA.)

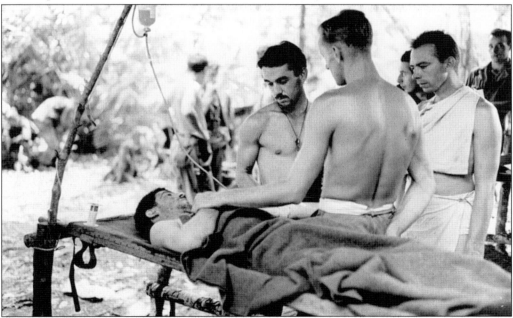

Major William L. Garlick of Baltimore (facing away from the camera), commander of the 3rd Portable Hospital of the 42nd General Hospital, gives plasma to a patient on New Guinea. The 3rd Portable Hospital entered the forward area from Brisbane during several New Guinea offensives to provide immediate medical assistance in heavy casualty zones. (Courtesy LoC, FSA-OWI Collection.)

Baltimore Sun correspondent Price Day covered the U.S. Fifth Army in Italy using two pigeons as couriers to relay reports from the front. Though slower than today's live streaming video, the pigeons were hardly inefficient, reportedly making 60 miles per hour! Shown here in May 1944 while covering action in the Garigliano Valley, Day is affixing a message capsule, which the pigeons carried on a leg. (Courtesy NARA.)

Baltimore lent its name to an entire class of heavy cruisers built during the war, starting with the lead ship, USS *Baltimore* (CA-68). The *Baltimore* participated in the invasions of the Gilberts, the Marianas, Iwo Jima, and Okinawa. She is shown here ready for action in September 1943, on her way to combat in the Pacific in dark sea-blue Measure 21 camouflage. (Courtesy NARA.)

Men of the 29th Infantry Division advance toward the front in or near St. Lo, France, on July 18, 1944. St. Lo had just been taken by the 29th Division. For its action in the vicinity of St. Lo, the 1st Battalion of the 175th was awarded the Distinguished Unit Citation and the French Croix de Guerre with Silver Gilt Star. The 175th Infantry Regiment, known before the war as the 5th Maryland Regiment and headquartered at the 5th Regiment Armory in Baltimore, was one of many units in which Baltimoreans fought and died during the liberation of Europe. (Courtesy NARA.)

The National Guard Association erected this memorial to D-Day participants atop one of the German gun emplacements that once defended Omaha Beach. Many Baltimoreans, including men of the 116th Infantry Regiment, 175th Infantry Regiment, and 104th Medical Battalion (the latter two headquartered in Baltimore), participated in the Normandy invasion and subsequent drive through France as part of the 29th Infantry Division. The 1st Battalion of the 116th landed in the first waves on Omaha Beach, most heavily defended and bloodiest of the invasion beaches. It suffered severe losses and earned a Distinguished Unit Citation and the French Croix de Guerre with Silver Gilt Star. The 1st Battalion of the 175th landed on Omaha the morning of June 7 and saw fierce action around St. Lo. Atop the emplacement is President Roosevelt's 1941 quote, "We too born to freedom and believing in freedom are willing to fight to maintain freedom. We and all others who believe as deeply as we do would rather die on our feet than live on our knees." (Author's collection.)

The 29th Infantry Division was composed of National Guard units from states once Union and Confederate, earning the nickname "Blue and Gray." Many of those units are represented on this plaque at the National Guard Monument on Omaha Beach. For its actions in Normandy, the entire 29th Division was awarded the French Croix de Guerre with a palm. (Author's collection.)

Men of the 175th Infantry Regiment, 29th Division, find themselves digging in amidst grave markers as they head into Germany in late October 1944, an eerie place to spend an evening even when not under fire. This photo was taken during the Siegfried Line Campaign, as the 175th advanced south toward the Hurtgen Forest region. (Courtesy NARA.)

Slogging through thick mud, men of the Baltimore-based 175th Infantry Regiment, 29th Infantry Division, march to the front through Aldenhoven, Germany, on November 21, 1944, the day the heavily defended town fell to the 29th Division. The town was taken during the 29th's advance toward the Hurtgen Forest. (Courtesy NARA.)

Men of Company F, 2nd Battalion, 175th Infantry Regiment, are pictured in the town of Goreleben, Germany, in May 1945. With them is honorary first sergeant "Ivan," a young Russian war orphan adopted by Company F and fully decked out in G.I. gear. The Cyrillic banner was a welcome to the Russian Army. (Courtesy NARA.)

Outnumbered by a swarm of German prisoners of war, these men of the 175th Infantry Regiment, 29th Infantry Division, seem to know that the end of the war is near—VE Day would come just five days later. These Germans, part of a V-2 rocket division across the Elbe from the American position, had negotiated a surrender en masse hoping to escape the rapidly advancing Soviet Army. It took two days to ferry all 10,367 across to American lines. By 1945, the Soviets were not in a forgiving mood, and Germans preferred to surrender to the other Allied powers whenever possible. The 29th captured a total of 38,912 prisoners by VE Day. (Courtesy NARA.)

Celebrating VE Day, infantrymen of the 175th Regiment, 29th Infantry Division, US XVI Corps, parade through the streets of Beckum, Germany, on May 8, 1945, as residents look on. It had been a long and bloody road for the Baltimore-based 175th and their fellow soldiers in the 29th Division. During the war, the 29th ranked second among all U.S. Army divisions in its number of sustained casualties, amounting to 19,814 men. (Courtesy NARA.)

Back home in Baltimore, the coming of VJ Day just 13 weeks later elicited these jubilant crowds of soldiers, sailors, and civilians scurrying up and down Howard Street amidst a flurry of American flags. The giant Stars and Stripes were raised by Hochschild Kohn and Company, along with a newly placed banner reading "Japan Now Beat, Thanks to Our Boys." Cars are jampacked along the road, with some people riding on top or alongside them. The war was finally over! (Courtesy the Maryland Historical Society.)

This wall of honor was erected in Dundalk Park and featured the names of all those from the community in the service of the armed forces. For some, the end of the war was bittersweet—not all returned home. (Courtesy the Dundalk–Patapsco Neck Historical Society.)

Selected Bibliography

Breihan, John R., Stan Piet, and Roger S. Mason. *Martin Aircraft 1909–1960.* Santa Ana, CA: Narkiewicz/Thompson, 1995.

Breihan, John R. "Wings of Democracy?" *From Mobtown to Charm City: New Perspectives on Baltimore's Past*, ed. Jessica Elfenbein, John R. Breihan, and Thomas L. Hollowak. Baltimore: Maryland Historical Society, 2002.

Bunker, John Gorley. *Liberty Ships: The Ugly Ducklings of World War II.* Annapolis: Naval Institute Press, 1972.

Churchill, Winston S. *The Hinge of Fate.* Boston: Houghton Mifflin Co., 1950.

Cooper, Sherod. *Liberty Ship: The Voyages of the* John W. Brown, *1942–1946.* Annapolis: Naval Institute Press, 1997.

Durr, Kenneth D. *Behind the Backlash: White Working-Class Politics in Baltimore, 1940–1980.* Chapel Hill: University of North Carolina Press, 2003.

———. "The Not-So Silent Majority: White Working Class Community." *From Mobtown to Charm City: New Perspectives on Baltimore's Past*, ed. Jessica Elfenbein, John R. Breihan, and Thomas L. Hollowak. Baltimore: Maryland Historical Society, 2002.

Gist, Robert S. *A History of Eastern Aircraft Corporation.* New York: William E. Rudge's Sons, 1944.

Manakee, Harold Randall, comp. *Maryland in World War II.* Volume I, *Military Participation.* Baltimore: Maryland Historical Society, War Records Division, 1950.

———. *Maryland in World War II.* Volume II, *Industry and Agriculture.* Baltimore: Maryland Historical Society, War Records Division, 1951.

———. *Maryland in World War II.* Volume III, *Home Front Volunteer Services.* Baltimore: Maryland Historical Society, War Records Division, 1958.

Risch, Erna. *The United States Army in World War II: The Technical Services: The Quartermaster Corps: Organization, Supply, and Services*, Volume 1. Washington, D.C.: Chief of Military History, 1953.

Rogers, Michael H., ed. *Answering Their Country's Call: Marylanders in World War II.* Baltimore: Johns Hopkins University Press, 2002.

Thompson, George Raynor, and Dixie R. Harris. *The United States Army in World War II: The Technical Services: The Signal Corps: The Outcome (Mid-1943 through 1945).* Washington, D.C.: Chief of Military History, 1966.

Wardlow, Chester. *The United States Army in World War II: The Technical Services: The Transportation Corps: Movements, Training, and Supply.* Washington, D.C.: Chief of Military History, 1951.

In addition to the above sources, factual information for this book was drawn from records of the Department of the Navy, the Coast Guard, and the Army Chief of Engineers at the National Archives in College Park; the Glenn L. Martin Papers at the Library of Congress; and the *Baltimore Sun* (select articles, 1936–1945), on microfilm at the University of Maryland–Baltimore County.